Plastic

Claire Llewellyn

SEA-TO-SEA
Mankato Collingwood London

This edition first published in 2006 by
Sea-to-Sea Publications
1980 Lookout Drive
North Mankato
Minnesota 56003

Copyright © Sea-to-Sea Publications 2006
Text copyright © Claire Llewellyn 2004, 2006

Printed in China

Library of Congress Cataloging-in-Publication Data

Llewellyn, Claire.
  Plastic/by Claire Llewellyn
    p. cm. — (I know that!)
  ISBN 1-932889-53-1
  1. Plastics—Juvenile literature. I. Title.

TA455.P5L58 2005
668.4—dc22

2004063710

9 8 7 6 5 4 3 2

Published by arrangement with the Watts Publishing Group Ltd, London

Series advisor: Gill Matthews, nonfiction literacy consultant and Inset trainer. Editor: Rachel Cooke.
Series design: Peter Scoulding. Designer: James Marks. Photography: Ray Moller unless otherwise credited.
Acknowledgments: Mark Antman /The Image Works/Topham: 14. Nick Cobbing/Still Pictures: 20.
Lauren Goodsmith/Image Works/Topham: 13t. Philippe Psaila/SPL: 16. Helene Rogers/Art Directors/Trip:12.
Joe Sohm/Image Works/Topham: 15l. Thanks to our models Jaydee Cozzi, Jakob Hawker, Hayley Sapsford,
and Phoebus Zavros.

Contents

Plastic is useful

Plastic is a very useful material.
All sorts of things are made
of plastic.

Food box

▼ *These things
are all made
of plastic.*

Comb

Sponge

Bracelet

Bag

Can you think of
three other
things that are
made of plastic?

Bottle

Toy

Cup

Ruler

Toothbrush

Watch

5

All kinds of plastic

There are many different kinds of plastic.

▶ *Plastic can be soft and bendy...*

▶ *or hard and stiff.*

Plastic can be squeezy...

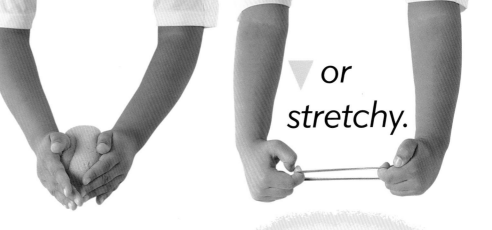

or stretchy.

It can be colorful...

What kinds of plastic have been used to make these swimming goggles?

or clear.

Plastic is strong

Plastic does not
break easily.
It is very strong.

► *A plastic bottle
does not break
when you drop it.*

This plastic basket holds a lot of laundry.

Have a look around your home. What things are made of plastic?

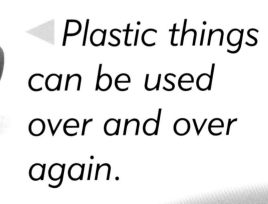

Plastic things can be used over and over again.

9

Plastic is waterproof

Water cannot get through plastic. It is a waterproof material.

Hood

Coat

Umbrella

Boots

▶ Plastic things keep you dry in the rain.

You can move water around in plastic.

Pour some drops of water on a paper towel. Now pour some drops on a plastic bag. What happens to the water?

Plastic is easy to look after

Plastic is easy to look after.
It does not need a lot of care.

▲ *Plastic chairs and tables do not rot.*

Plastic toys never get rusty.

Many outdoor things are made of plastic. How many can you spot at school?

This plastic-covered cloth is easy to clean.

13

Plastic is made from oil

People make plastic from oil.

Plastic is not a natural material. It is made by people, not by nature.

▲ *Black, sticky oil is found under the ground.*

▼ *The oil is taken to a big factory.*

▲ *Some of the oil is used to make tiny plastic chips.*

Shaping plastic

Plastic melts when it is heated. It can then be made into different shapes.

► *This is a mold for making plastic bricks. Melted plastic has been poured into it.*

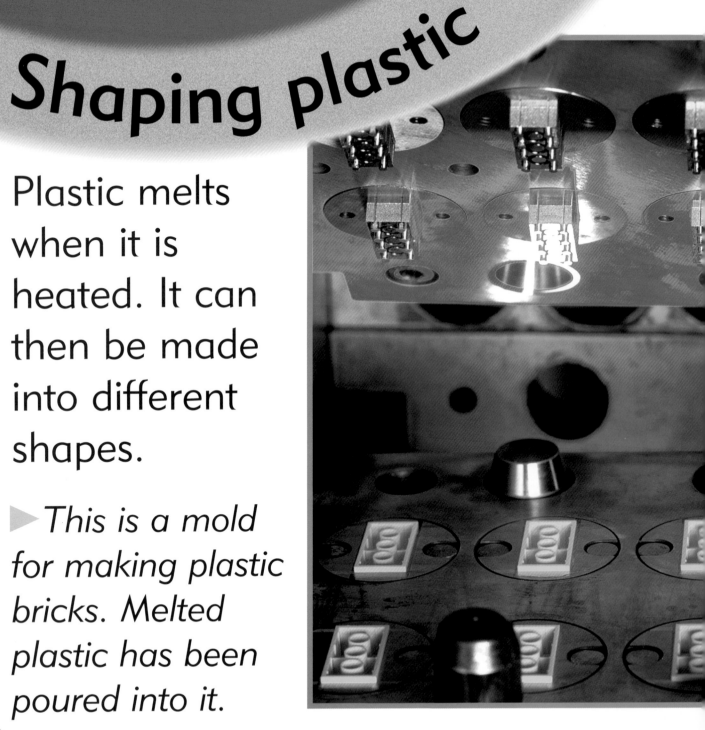

As the plastic cooled it went hard. It has kept the brick shape of the mold.

We pour hot, runny gelatin into a mold. What happens as the gelatin cools?

These things were made in molds.

Wearing plastic

Hot plastic can be pulled into long, thin threads. These are used to make cloth.

▼ *All these clothes were made from plastic.*

Soft, stretchy cardigan

Soft, fluffy fleece

Do you think any of your clothes are made from plastic?

Smooth, strong skirt

Smooth, stretchy leotards

19

Plastic makes trash

A lot of plastic ends up as trash. We must try to throw less away.

► *Look at all the plastic in this trash can.*

These empty plastic cartons and pots are too useful to be trash. How could you use them again?

▲ *Don't throw away a plastic bottle! Use it again.*

I know that...

1 Plastic is useful.

2 There are many kinds of plastic

3 Plastic is strong.

4 Plastic is waterproof.

5 Plastic is easy to look after.

6 Plastic is made from oil.

7 Plastic can be shaped when it is melted. It goes hard when it is cool.

8 Plastic is used to make cloth.

9 We must try to throw away less plastic.

Index

About this book

I Know That! is designed to introduce children to the process of gathering information and using reference books, one of the key skills needed to begin more formal learning at school. For this reason, each book's structure reflects the information books children will use later in their learning career—with key information in the main text and additional facts and ideas in the captions. The panels give an opportunity for further activities, ideas, or discussions. The contents page and index are helpful reference guides.

The language is carefully chosen to be accessible to children just beginning to read. Illustrations support the text but also give information in their own right; active consideration and discussion of images is another key referencing skill. The main aim of the series is to build confidence—showing children how much they already know and giving them the ability to gather new information for themselves. With this in mind, the *I know that...* section at the end of the book is a simple way for children to revisit what they already know as well as what they have learned from reading the book.